Next Door
SAVIOR

GROUP STUDY
LEADER'S GUIDE

MAX LUCADO

with

DAVE VEERMAN AND LEN WOODS

W PUBLISHING GROUP™

www.wpublishinggroup.com

A Division of Thomas Nelson, Inc.
www.ThomasNelson.com

Published by W Publishing Group, a Division of Thomas Nelson, Inc., P.O. Box 141000, Nashville, Tennessee 37214.

Scripture quotations are taken from the following sources:

Scripture quotations marked (AMP) are taken from The Amplified Bible. Copyright © 1954, 1958, 1962, 1964, 1965, 1987 by the Lockman Foundation. All rights reserved. Used by permission. Scripture quotations marked (CEV) are taken from The Contemporary English Version. Copyright © 1995 by the American Bible Society. Scripture quotations marked (GNT) are taken from the Good News Translation, Second Edition, formerly known as Good News Bible in Today's English Version, copyright © 1992 by the American Bible Society. Used by permission. All rights reserved. Scripture quotations marked (MSG) are taken from the The Message, copyright © 1993, 1994, 1995, 1996, 2000, 2001, 2002. Used by permission of NavPress Publishing Group. Scripture quotations marked (NASB) are taken from the New American Standard Bible,® copyright © 1960, 1962, 1963, 1968, 1971, 1972, 1973, 1975, 1977, 1995 by the Lockman Foundation. Used by permission. Scripture quotations marked (NCV) are taken from The New Century Version, copyright © 1987, 1988, 1991 by Word Publishing, a Division of Thomas Nelson, Inc. Used by permission. Scripture quotations marked (NIV) are taken from the Holy Bible, New International Version®, copyright © 1973, 1978, 1984 by the International Bible Society. Used by permission of Zondervan Bible Publishing House. All rights reserved. The "NIV" and "New International Version" trademarks are registered in the United States Patent and Trademark Office by International Bible Society. Use of either trademark requires the permission of the International Bible Society. Scripture quotations marked (NKJV) are taken from The New King James Version, copyright ©1979, 1980, 1982 by Thomas Nelson, Inc. Used by permission. All rights reserved. Scripture quotations marked (NLT) are taken from The Holy Bible, New Living Translation, copyright © 1996. Used by permission of Tyndale House Publishers, Inc, Wheaton, Illinois 60189. All rights reserved. Scripture quotations marked (TLB) are taken from The Living Bible, copyright © 1971. Used by permission of Tyndale House Publishers, Inc., Wheaton, Illinois 60189. Scripture quotations marked (NRSV) are taken from the New Revised Standard Version Bible, copyright © 1989 by the Division of Christian Education of the National Council of the Churches of Christ in the U.S.A. Used by permission. All rights reserved.

Produced with the assistance of The Livingstone Corporation (www.LivingstoneCorporation.com). Project staff includes Dave Veerman and Mary Horner Collins.

ISBN 0-8499-4521-6

Printed in the United States of America

04 05 06 07 PHX 9 8 7 6 5 4 3 2 1

Contents

SESSIONS:

Note to the Leader

Thank you for accepting the challenge of leading a small group through this *Next Door Savior* study. Although we've included a box of resources to make your job easier, it will still involve a healthy investment on your part. But we're confident that your investment will be infinitely rewarding. We pray along with you that participants in this study will gain a deeper understanding of the Incarnation and a greater love for Christ.

As you unpack these materials and think about this study, here are a few points to remember.

Preparation

As the Boy Scout motto says, "Be prepared." This begins on a personal level as you familiarize yourself with the sessions, the DVD/VHS, and the other resources. Take time to watch all the video clips of Max and the testimonies as you work through the lesson plans. Then you won't be caught by surprise in any session.

Good preparation also means being prepared spiritually. Ask God to give you insight and guidance as you lead, and begin now to pray for your group, even if you don't yet know the specific participants.

Before leading each session, watch the "Leader's Edge" segment for that session. That's where Max gives encouragement and teaching tips for a specific session. Next, work through the session yourself, watching the video at the right points and answering the questions. Be sure to read the "Leader's Notes" in the shaded boxes and highlight those that you want to remember.

Just before each session, make sure your DVD or video equipment is in working order and turned on with the volume at the proper level. Then all you have to do is hit one button to begin. Think through the physical environment and see that the lighting and seating are comfortable, so everyone will be able to see the video screen. Answer these questions: Do you have room near the screen to sit (or stand) and lead? Can you bring latecomers into the back of the room so they don't disrupt the group? Is the lighting bright enough for writing but not too bright for the screen (or should you dim the lights when showing a video)? Is there a clock in the room so that you will know the time as the meeting progresses? Do you have all the needed materials (extra Bibles, pencils/pens, etc.)?

If you plan on having refreshments (great for facilitating informal interaction), make sure they don't become a distraction. Imagine, for example, discussing an important principle near the end of the session and then smelling fresh popcorn being made—the group's attention would be quickly diverted!

In short, the best way to prepare is to think through every aspect of the meeting, from greeting people at the door to saying good-bye.

Timing

Each session is designed to run between 45 and 60 minutes. If, for example, you use this for an adult Sunday school class, you may have limited time to teach before everyone has to rush off for worship, choir, or gathering their kids. In that case, you will want to keep each section of the session concise.

You will see suggested timing in parentheses after each section title, for example: *"Open House (6 to 9 minutes)."* All of the first numbers ("6") when added together total 45 minutes; all of the second numbers ("9") total 60 minutes. So if your time is limited, you will be able to get through the whole session as you watch the clock and follow those times.

The times for each section also give you an indication of how to pace the session. Some group leaders make the mistake of spending so much time on the opening questions that they don't have time for the ending questions. Don't shortchange the group. Even if everyone is having a great time sharing stories at the beginning, you will need to stop and move to the next section. Otherwise, you will run out of time and interest at the end when you're emphasizing application.

Setup

As already mentioned, the physical setting affects the group and their willingness to discuss. The room should be warm and inviting. (We suggest having the *Next Door Savior* CD playing in the background as everyone enters.) For a larger group or Sunday school class, you may want to assign greeters to make everyone feel welcomed.

As you lead and teach, try to exude warmth—be open, inviting, positive, and enthusiastic. That's one of Max Lucado's strengths in the DVD/VHS sessions—when he speaks, you feel as though he is talking just to you and not preaching to the multitude.

The Guides

Undoubtedly you've already discovered that your *Next Door Savior* Group Study Kit contains two workbooks that look very similar: the *Participant's Guide* and the *Leader's Guide.* You've found the *Leader's Guide;* otherwise you wouldn't be reading this. We've made them look alike so that group members won't be intimidated by your "inside information." The *Leader's Guide* contains the complete *Participant's Guide* with the same sections, questions, and page numbers. The difference between the two books is that the *Leader's Guide* also has helpful resource material in the front, the "lesson goal" for each session, suggested times for each section, and shaded boxes with leader's notes.

You will need one *Participant's Guide* for each group member. You may purchase them at your local bookstore or call toll-free 1-800-933-9673.

Discussion

Because the *Participant's Guide* has been written for use in a group *or* individually, all the questions have space for the answers. At times you will want to discuss the questions and let participants take notes in the space provided. Sometimes you may have the group write their answers and then share what they have written. And at other times, you may want to have everyone write down their responses privately. *Decide this beforehand,* during your preparation time. Also, feel free to skip questions if you need the time.

As you lead the discussion, remember

- Accept what each person says, without making judgments. You may want to probe further, but don't give a person the idea that what he or she has just said is totally off base or "stupid." If the discussion seems to be taking a wrong turn, stop and explain how you feel; then get it back on track.

- Keep the discussion moving along. Each session has many questions, so don't get hung up on one, especially at the beginning.

- Work at getting the whole group involved. Don't let one or two people dominate the discussion because they are more articulate or because they have a personal agenda. Give everyone a chance to contribute.

- This is a discussion, not a speech, so don't add your two cents' worth after every comment.

- Keep the focus on Christ and on the lesson—it's not about you. More on leading discussions is included in the Small Group Toolbox section.

Wrap-Up/Assignments

Some leaders find it helpful to give participants an assignment at the end of each session. This can help the main points of the lesson come alive. Ideas for possible assignments are included for many of the lessons. If you give an assignment, be sure to talk about it as you begin the next session. This brings some accountability and recognition to the group.

Frequently Asked Questions

Do I have to read the *Next Door Savior* book to understand the study guide/DVD/VHS course?

No, but the book adds more detail and gives a fuller discussion of the materials found on the DVD/VHS. The eight sessions in the study guide and companion DVD/VHS highlight only about one-third of the book.

Do I have to have special training to lead this study guide/DVD/VHS course?

No, but you need to be prepared.

Does a person have to do this study as part of a small group?

It's not necessary, but we recommend it. As the old saying goes, "Sorrows shared are sorrows halved. Joys shared are joys doubled." The Christian life was meant to be lived in community. We learn from others. We need others. God made us to help each other, encourage each other, and spur on one another to love and good deeds (see Hebrews 10:23–25).

Some of the questions in this guide are rather personal. I can't see myself or others being this vulnerable with a whole group.

That's fine. No one should ever be coerced to reveal things they are uncomfortable revealing. Understand, however, that one of the devil's most effective strategies is to persuade us that our problems are unique and that no one else will understand (or, worse yet, that others will be horrified). By convincing people to be overly secretive, by getting folks to hide their true selves from each other, the enemy succeeds at keeping hurting souls from finding hope and healing. As you and the group members answer the questions in this study guide, make it your goal and encourage everyone to either be silent or be honest. If you *do* decide to respond, resist the urge to give safe, superficial church answers. Be real. Others will be encouraged by your authenticity.

Is it necessary to use the DVD/VHS each time we gather?

No, this study guide (though containing references to the DVD/VHS) can stand alone and work by itself. The DVD/VHS teaching segments and testimonies are provided only as a tool to enhance your group's learning experience.

Small Group Toolbox

Our Questions

"My group won't discuss! We gather and everyone is as talkative as can be while we're eating snacks and drinking coffee. But then we go into our official meeting time, and the whole dynamic changes! People clam up. Or they give shallow answers. How do I get my group to really *wrestle* with God's Word? What can I do to liven up our discussion times?"

Ever feel like this? If so, you're not alone. "Dull discussions" are one of the most frequent complaints of group leaders. Fortunately, you can learn to use good questions wisely. You have the tools, and there *are* some commonsense rules for getting others to open up.

The Law of Preparation. On any given study group night, there are countless questions you *could* ask. But there are far fewer questions you *should* ask, and only a handful of questions that you will have *time* to ask. So plan ahead. Think creatively and pray earnestly. Ask God to help you choose and tailor questions to where the group is collectively and to where folks are individually.

The Warmup Rule. People are more willing to tackle deep questions if they have first had the chance to bounce around some less threatening questions. Toss out the lighter icebreaker questions (provided in the *Open House* section of each lesson) so the group can adequately warm up.

The Chill Out Axiom. What to do? Your study guide has six full pages of great questions. How can you possibly get through them all in 45 minutes (or an hour at most)? Guess what? You can't. And that's okay. Three or four good questions that spark deep introspection and meaningful interaction are better than racing through ten or twelve queries.

The Patience Principle. Consider for a moment the Q&A portion of beauty pageants. Usually the questions are somewhat profound (for example, "How would you solve the problem of terrorism?" or "What advice would you give to a young girl who thinks she's unattractive?"). Yet the contestants are supposed to answer *immediately*—and they invariably do—in canned, sappy sound bites.

This is *not* the dynamic we're looking for in your *Next Door Savior* group study! Good questions that probe the deepest mysteries of life take time to process. We can't expect people to grapple with God's truth, peer into their own souls, and articulate thoughtfully—all in a minute or two. Be okay with periods of silence, and let the group know that thinking before speaking is perfectly acceptable (and actually desirable).

The No Agenda Tenet. Beware of the temptation to use questions as a manipulative tool to browbeat people into a prearranged destination. To borrow courtroom terminology, don't "lead the witness." Resist the urge to play the role of "junior Holy Spirit." Trust, instead, that God will illumine hearts and lead people into truth. Like good tools, your questions should function as a helpful spade or a flashlight, never a sledgehammer.

The Listen Up Dictum. Picture this scenario: A leader throws out a good question to the group. Some brave soul takes a stab at it, others in the group ponder if and how they will answer, while the leader scrambles mentally and looks ahead at the workbook, wondering what question he or she will try next. In other words, *no one is listening!*

This dreadful habit forgets that the goal in asking questions is not only to get group members to ponder God's truth and wrestle with applying it to their own lives, but also *to gain insight into where your fellow group members are* so that you can better understand them, help them, pray for them, and encourage them. Baring one's soul before others can be risky and scary. With this in mind, we need to honor people with our full attention. And we need to encourage the group to do the same.

The Fairness Doctrine. Simply stated, we should never ask our group any question that we're not willing to answer honestly ourselves.

These are only a few observations about the question of questions. The bottom line is, the more we work at learning to draw people out, the better our small group experiences will be.

The "One Anothers"

What does a healthy group study community look like? What is our job description each time we gather to undertake this study of the *Next Door Savior?*

The following instructions from the Bible give us some guidelines about how to be a caring community:

- Love one another. (John 13:34–35)
- Be devoted to one another. (Romans 12:10)
- Rejoice and mourn with one another. (Romans 12:15)
- Live in harmony with one another. (Romans 12:16)
- Stop judging one another. (Romans 14:13)
- Accept one another. (Romans 15:7)
- Instruct one another. (Romans 15:14)
- Be humble toward one another. (1 Corinthians 4:6)
- Be considerate of one another. (1 Corinthians 11:33)
- Have concern for one another. (1 Corinthians 12:25)
- Serve one another in love. (Galatians 5:13)
- Bear the burdens of one another. (Galatians 6:2)
- Be patient with one another. (Ephesians 4:2)
- Forgive one another. (Ephesians 4:32)
- Be kind to one another. (Ephesians 4:32)
- Be honest with one another. (Colossians 3:9)
- Encourage one another. (1 Thessalonians 5:11)
- Spur on one another to love and good deeds. (Hebrews 10:24)
- Confess sins to one another. (James 5:16)
- Pray for one another. (James 5:16)
- Offer hospitality to one another. (1 Peter 4:9)
- Treat one another with humility. (1 Peter 5:5)

Roles in a Group Study

Remember those potluck dinners in the church basement? Every now and then the pickings were slim because not enough people contributed or because everyone decided to bring the same dish. But most of the time you got to feast on a wide and bountiful selection of home-prepared salads, casseroles, and desserts. The meal was much better when *everybody* contributed something.

This principle is certainly true in the context of group studies. Good groups become solid, at least in part, when every member does his or her part and makes a contribution. The ministry load is spread around. Everybody is doing something. Each member is needed and has a vital contribution to make. It's "our group." In such a group, every individual feels protective of the group. Members become boosters.

Contrast that with the group where one person does *everything*. It's "the leader's group." He or she is a one-man or one-woman show—teaching, hosting, leading the prayer time, and organizing social events. Everyone else feels like dead weight. They show up and watch. They fill chairs but feel no sense of ownership. Over time, uninvolved spectators become disinterested, often critical.

To keep this dynamic from developing, to make your group a healthy body where each member is doing his or her part, you can assign some group roles. Here are some suggestions:

Prayer Captain—keeps up with needs and leads the group's prayer time

Social Coordinator—plans occasional fun get-togethers (as per the group's wishes)

Refreshment Guru—helps organize snacks and drinks (assuming the group wants to include this as part of their regular meeting)

Outreach Leader—provides direction for the group's efforts to invite and include new folks who need to meet the next door Savior

You may also want to rotate the responsibility of leading the discussion time.

There are other possibilities, but the point is to get folks involved by doing something more than just showing up. Remember, people tend to go where they feel needed and useful, and they do their best when they are functioning in areas where they have real passion.

Suggested Memory Verses

Session One: Introduction to Next Door Savior
And the Word became flesh and lived among us, and we have seen his glory, the glory as of a father's only son, full of grace and truth. (John 1:14 NRSV)

Session Two: Jesus . . . Your Next Door Savior
For in Christ there is all of God in a human body. (Colossians 2:9 TLB)

Session Three: Jesus . . . Knows How You Feel
Because he himself suffered when he was tempted, he is able to help those who are being tempted. (Hebrews 2:18 NIV)

Session Four: Jesus . . . Near Enough to Touch
As the sun went down that evening, people throughout the village brought sick family members to Jesus. No matter what their diseases were, the touch of his hand healed every one. (Luke 4:40 NLT)

Session Five: Jesus . . . Strong Enough to Trust
Jesus answered, "I am the way and the truth and the life. No one comes to the Father except through me." (John 14:6 NIV)

Session Six: Jesus . . . Carried Our Sins
Christ carried our sins in his body on the cross so we would stop living for sin and start living for what is right. (1 Peter 2:24 NCV)

Session Seven: Jesus . . . Speaks for You
Jesus understands every weakness of ours, because he was tempted in every way that we are. But he did not sin! So whenever we are in need, we should come bravely before the throne of our merciful God. There we will be treated with undeserved kindness, and we will find help. (Hebrews 4:15–16 CEV)

Session Eight: Jesus . . . Give It All to Him

Come to me, all you who are weary and burdened, and I will give you rest. (Matthew 11:28 NIV)

Introduction

Welcome to the *Next Door Savior* group study! This multimedia resource has been created to help you better understand and more fully embrace the stunning truth of the Incarnation—God's coming to earth and becoming one of us; Jesus of Nazareth, the perfect God-man. At the end of this experience, our desire is that you might be convinced that Jesus is "near enough to touch, strong enough to trust." But beyond just knowing more about the Lord, our hope is that you will love him more passionately, appreciate him more deeply, and live for him more consistently.

Certainly an individual may use this material; however, we believe it will be most effective when used in a group setting. The simple truth is this: God created us for relationship—deep friendship with himself and with other people. Isn't this what Jesus meant when he declared the most important goal in life is to love God with all our being and to love our neighbors as ourselves (Mark 12:28–31)? God designed us for *life in community.* He means for us to live and grow *together with others.* In the same way a person can't be married alone, it's also impossible to be a Christian all by yourself. We need the spiritual encouragement and support of the body of Christ. And we need to spur on other believers by our faith (Hebrews 10:23–25). That's why the content and format of this study are geared to Sunday school classes, men's or women's Bible studies, neighborhood outreach groups, and other adult discussion groups.

The components of each session are the same throughout. In each lesson you will find:

Open House—a warmup question or two to facilitate group interaction and to help the group begin thinking about the big idea of the session.

At Home with Max—a Bible study/discussion introduced by Max Lucado on the companion DVD/VHS. In this portion of the session, we'll monitor closely the amazing words and mind-boggling works of this man named Jesus who has "moved into the neighborhood." What exactly is he up to? Why is he here? What does he want from us?

Front Porch Story—an introduction to some real people who have been touched and transformed by the Savior.

Home Improvement—a few questions for personal application and some journal pages intended to get you to live for (and like) Jesus Christ, our next door Savior.

Community Connection—useful tools from the *Next Door Savior* curriculum kit and other materials that can enhance your relationship with God.

Bonus Music Performance—At the end of each of the VHS tapes and included on each DVD you'll notice a live recording of one of the songs from the *Next Door Savior* music CD. They are titled "Next Door Savior performed by Warren Barfield" and "Live With Us performed by Warren Barfield." These can be used in a variety of ways. You may want to have one of these songs playing as walk-in music for your group, or you may choose to use the songs as they tie in to a particular session. They are there for your use and enjoyment.

When the apostle John summarized the reason he wrote his biography of Christ (the fourth Gospel of the New Testament) he said, "Jesus did many other miraculous signs in the presence of his disciples, which are not recorded in this book. But these are written that you may believe that Jesus is the Christ, the Son of God, and that by believing you may have life in his name" (John 20:30–31 NIV).

That's an apt description of this *Next Door Savior* project too. Jesus said and did much more than what you will discover in this short study guide. But the selected incidents and highlighted lessons are more than enough to deepen your faith and to guide you to a richer life.

Make that your prayer as we begin!

Session One

Introduction to *Next Door Savior*

Lesson Goal: To introduce the *Next Door Savior* concept. As a result of this session, participants will understand that God really *did* step out of eternity into time. He left the splendor of heaven, and he moved in, so to speak, right next door. And why? Because he loves to be with the ones he loves.

Study Overview *(7 to 10 minutes)*

Play the "Next Door Savior" theme song from the CD as everyone gets seated.

If this is the first time this group has been together, spend a few minutes getting to know each other.

Play the video clip on the DVD/VHS titled "Study Overview." It features Max and a few pastors from the advisory board discussing why this topic is important, an overview of the format for the sessions, and a music video of the "Next Door Savior" song, with clips from various sessions. The clip lasts about six minutes.

Open House *(6 to 9 minutes)*

What do you like best about your hometown? In your opinion, what is your hometown's greatest claim to fame?

Spend a few moments imagining what it might be like to be a next door neighbor to the following kinds of people. Discuss your ideas.

Although this is not a discussion question per se, you could ask how they might imagine their neighbors responding to some of the characters listed below:

- a CIA agent
- an exotic dancer
- an all-pro athlete
- a Hollywood A-list actor
- a person with AIDS
- a publisher of pornographic magazines
- a U.S. senator
- a televangelist
- an Elvis impersonator

Think back over the various neighbors you've had over the years. Who have been some of your favorite neighbors? Why did you enjoy them? What qualities make a good neighbor?

At Home with Max (14 to 17 minutes)

At this time, show the DVD/VHS video segment for Session One in which Max introduces the series. It's short—only about two minutes long.

This study focuses on one question: Who is this one called Jesus? This carpenter from Nazareth was certainly unique and kept doing "God things." What do we do in the face of his astounding works and his amazing words?

Read how Jesus is described in a very famous passage from the New Testament:

He is the image of the invisible God, the firstborn over all creation. For by him all things were created: things in heaven and on earth, visible and invisible, whether thrones or powers or rulers or authorities; all things were created by him and for him. He is before all things, and in him all things hold together. And he is the head of the body, the church; he is the beginning and the firstborn from among the dead, so that in everything he might have the supremacy. For God was pleased to have all his fullness dwell in him, and through him to reconcile to himself all things, whether things on earth or things in heaven, by making peace through his blood, shed on the cross. (Colossians 1:15–20 NIV)

What descriptive phrases in this paragraph indicate Jesus is more than a mere man?

Answers could include the following: "He is the image of the invisible God, the firstborn over all creation"; "by him all things were created"; "all things were created by him and for him"; "he is before all things"; "in him all things hold together"; "he is the head of the body, the church"; "he is the beginning and the firstborn from among the dead"; "in everything he might have the supremacy"; "God was pleased to have all his fullness dwell in him, and through him to reconcile to himself all things."

Which statement or declaration from this passage really jumps out at you? Why?

Another famous Bible passage about Jesus Christ is found in a short book called Philippians. Here's the entire context:

In your lives you must think and act like Christ Jesus. Christ himself was like God in everything. But he did not think that being equal with God was something to be used for his own benefit. But he gave up his place with God and made himself nothing. He was born to be a man and became like a servant. And when he was living as a man, he humbled himself and was fully obedient to God, even when that caused his death—death on a cross. *So God raised him to the highest place. God made his name greater than every other name so that every knee will bow to the name of Jesus—everyone in heaven, on earth, and under the earth. And everyone will confess that Jesus Christ is Lord and bring glory to God the Father.* (2:5–11 NCV, emphasis added)

How does this passage (especially the emphasized section) describe Jesus Christ? What was his attitude? What surprising actions did he choose? Why do you think he acted as he did?

What must it have been like for Christ to leave the splendor and perfection of heaven to come and live in our sin-ravaged world?

Here's one more classic passage that speaks of the Incarnation—God's becoming man in Christ:

> *In the beginning was the Word, and the Word was with God, and the Word was God. He was in the beginning with God. All things came into being through him, and without him not one thing came into being. What has come into being in him was life, and the life was the light of all people. The light shines in the darkness, and the darkness did not overcome it. . . .*
>
> *The true light, which enlightens everyone, was coming into the world. He was in the world, and the world came into being through him; yet the world did not know him. He came to what was his own, and his own people did not accept him. But to all who received him, who believed in his name, he gave power to become children of God, who were born, not of blood or of the will of the flesh or of the will of man, but of God. And the Word became flesh and lived among us, and we have seen his glory, the glory as of a father's only son, full of grace and truth.* (John 1:1–5, 9–14 NRSV)

In this passage, John focuses on "the Word." What phrases and terms comprise his description of "the Word"?

Possible answers: "the Word was with God"; "the Word was God"; "He was in the beginning with God"; "All things came into being through him"; "What has come into being in him was life, and the life was the light of all people"; "He was in the world, and the world came into being through him; yet the world did not know him"; "to all who received him, who believed in his name, he gave power to become children of God"; "the Word became flesh and lived among us."

To whom or what is this passage referring when it speaks of "the Word"? How do you know?

What does it mean that the Word is "full of grace and truth"?

This passage gives explicit insight into what makes a person a true child of God. Summarize what it says.

Front Porch Story (6 to 9 minutes)

This opening session has no testimony on the DVD/VHS; therefore, it might be an optimal time to share your own experience of how you met Christ and how he is changing your life.

Or, you could divide the group into pairs and have them share their spiritual journeys with each other.

[There is no video testimony for this session.]

Home Improvement (12 to 15 minutes)

If the Bible passages we've been looking at are true (and we believe they are), then on a certain date in history, in an actual place, the Creator literally stepped out of eternity into time—right into his own creation. God moved into earth's neighborhood. He became close enough to touch!

Is this a new thought to you? What questions does this fact spark in your mind?

Think about your mental picture of Jesus. What five adjectives or phrases best describe how you viewed Jesus when you were growing up? Where do you think you got this notion of Christ?

How has your view of Christ changed over the years?

Write an honest prayer in the space provided. Tell God what you're thinking and feeling as you begin this *Next Door Savior* experiment. What questions do you have? What needs?

Take time for everyone to write privately and quietly, then close in prayer.

Optional Assignment: Tell them to visit two neighbors and take a "survey." Regardless of how well they know their neighbors, they should ask three of the following questions:

- Recall your house or where you lived when you were a child (under ten years old). What was the neighborhood like?
- Where did you live before you came here?
- What do you like best about our neighborhood?
- What could we do to improve our neighborhood?
- Which neighbors do you know best? Why?

Community Connection

- Listen to the title track on the *Next Door Savior* CD. It's a great song that beautifully summarizes the theme of this study.
- Read the Gospel of Mark in one sitting. You can probably do it in 35 or 45 minutes. It's the shortest account of the life of the Christ—and also the most action-packed.
- See if your church library has a copy of *The Visual Bible.* If so, check it out. This video version of Matthew's Gospel depicts Jesus in a way you've never seen.

Journaling Page

Journaling Page

Session Two

Jesus . . . Your Next Door Savior

Lesson Goal: To realize our need for a God-man Savior. As a result of this session, participants will know that the *God-man* Jesus knows us through and through and can bring us to God.

Open House (7 to 10 minutes)

Play the "Next Door Savior" theme song as you begin.

Briefly review the last session before heading into this one. If you gave the assignment, ask how it went.

What Jesus movies or Jesus paintings are you familiar with? Which one is your favorite? Which one do you like the least? Why?

Overall, what is your impression of these assorted artistic representations of Christ?

When in your life have you been most amazed or mystified by Jesus? What happened?

At Home with Max *(18 to 22 minutes)*

This video segment is about 10 minutes long.

In the DVD/VHS teaching segment, Max focuses on a question Jesus asked his followers. It is a profound question, arguably the single most important inquiry in all of life. More important, it is the question Christ continues to ask of every person on the planet: "Who do you say I am?" (Matthew 16:15 NIV).

To answer that question well, we have to engage in a kind of neighborhood watch. We have to focus our attention on Jesus, this strange newcomer to earth's community. We have to keep an eye on him. Who is he? What is he up to? Why is he here? What does he want?

Jesus aimed this piercing query at his original followers right on the heels of a shocking incident. Christ had, without warning, disrupted a funeral procession. He had . . . well, let's allow the Bible to speak for itself:

> *He went up and touched the coffin, and those carrying it stood still. He said, "Young man, I say to you, get up!" The dead man sat up and began to talk, and Jesus gave him back to his mother.* (Luke 7:14–15 NIV)

If you've been a long-term churchgoer or Bible reader—if you've been exposed repeatedly to the New Testament stories of Jesus—it is easy to become blasé about his words and works. Read this entire passage again (Luke 7:11–17). Try to see this funeral through new eyes, as though for the first time. Put yourself there among the mourners. Feel their grief. Then watch what Jesus does. Listen to his words. A dead boy becomes "undead" right before your eyes. Now, how do you respond?

If you have time, have everyone read the passage silently.

How did this incident demonstrate Jesus' humanity? What did it reveal about his divinity?

In Mark 4, we have a record of another incident in which a just-awakened Jesus stilled a raging storm. How did the disciples respond? "They were terrified and asked each other, 'Who is this? Even the wind and the waves obey him!'" (Mark 4:41 NIV).

Imagine being with Peter and the rest of the men in the boat during this storm. The passage says the disciples were "terrified."

Do you think they were more frightened by the rough weather, or by the presence of the One who commanded the weather? Expand on that one word *terrified* and try to express the jumble of emotions and thoughts that must have been in their hearts and minds.

Above we mentioned Matthew 16:15, that crucial moment when Jesus asked his disciples for the grapevine report on himself. In so many words he was asking: "What's the buzz on me? What are folks saying? Who or what do they think I am?" Then the point-blank query: "But what about *you*? Who do *you* say I am?"

On the DVD/VHS, Max explained how he pictured this scene. How do you imagine it?

The Gospels make no big secret of the fact that the disciples were a flaky, shaky bunch (at least until *after* Christ rose from the dead!). Devoted one day, they doubted the next. In the instance above, Peter stumbled into the right answer. Yet in the days and weeks to come, he would make *plenty* of wrong choices.

Why is steady faith in Christ so difficult? And living by faith even harder?

How does it make you feel to realize that even the so-called "giants of the faith" (that is, believers like the apostle Peter) struggled to come to terms with the identity of Jesus?

Colossians 2:9 declares, "For in Christ there is all of God in a human body" (TLB). What does this verse reveal about the true identity of Jesus? Why is it difficult to process this statement and the other truths we're studying?

Front Porch Story (10 to 13 minutes)
A Neighbor's Love—Blake Hightower
Watch Blake Hightower's testimony on the DVD/VHS.

This should take about six minutes. The testimony is powerful, so be prepared for tears. In fact, you may want to have a time of silent reflection after which you wrap up with a gentle verbal challenge to the group and close in prayer.

Where did Willie find the compassion to love such an unlovable, hardhearted guy as Blake?

Did God use other people to draw you to himself? If so, in what way?

A simple lawn mower—that is what God used to reveal his love and grace to Blake Hightower. What do you have that God can use to introduce the next door Savior to your neighbors?

Optional Assignment: Spend some time walking around your neighborhood. Imagine Jesus "moving in" next door or up the street. Based on what you already know about Jesus, describe what you think he might do, how he might live.

Pray for your neighbors. Ask God to make himself real to them. Ask him to show you how he wants to use you to introduce folks to Jesus—our next door Savior.

Home Improvement (10 to 15 minutes)

Somebody slips some sodium pentothol (truth serum) into your morning coffee and thirty minutes later asks you, "Who do you believe Jesus is?" What kind of raw, unedited thoughts do you think would come out of your mouth? (Note: Don't answer in the way you think you're *supposed* to answer—respond according to what's really in the deepest recesses of your heart and mind. What do you honestly think about the carpenter from Galilee? Was he a good man, a prophet, a victim of circumstances, a faith-healer, a wise teacher, or what?)

Circle the titles or descriptions of Jesus below that mean the most to you, and then describe why they are meaningful.

Savior	Master
Lord	Lamb of God
Lord of lords	Good Shepherd
Christ/Messiah	Holy One of God
Friend of sinners	Son of Man
King of kings	Healer
Judge	Redeemer
Rabbi	Other:
Great Physician	

Community Connection

- Listen to "I Surrender All" on the *Next Door Savior* CD.
- If you haven't already, begin reading the book *Next Door Savior*. It gives a fuller treatment of the ideas we are discussing here.
- Check out the book mentioned by Blake Hightower, *God Came Near*, by Max Lucado.

Journaling Page

Session Three

Jesus . . . Knows How You Feel

Lesson Goal: To know that Jesus has experienced what it means to be human—all the pain and all the testing. As a result of this session, participants will realize that God understands us fully.

Open House (7 to 9 minutes)

Play the "Next Door Savior" theme song as you begin.

Briefly review the last session before heading into this one. If you gave the assignment, ask how it went.

If you know it, tell the group a bit about your ancestry.

What noble, famous (or infamous) forefathers or foremothers are in your family tree, if any?

Looking back over your life, what do you see as three or four key events or defining moments?

An unwed mother. A barn in Bethlehem. A handful of suspect witnesses. Why do you think Jesus—"God with skin on"—made his entrance into the world in such a nondescript way, in such a "Podunk place," and under such eyebrow-raising circumstances?

If you were writing the story of the universe and were devising a way for a loving deity to rescue a doomed humanity, how might your version differ from God's?

At Home with Max (17 to 21 minutes)

Show video segment three here. It will take about thirteen minutes.

Our focus in this session is on Christ's full humanity. Heaven's highest King didn't just "put in an appearance," he moved in! He left glory and made this fallen world his home—for more than thirty years. As a result, he truly knows what we're up against. He experienced the full gamut of what it means to be human. The phrase you need to fix in your head and heart is: *He's been there; he knows how I feel.*

On the DVD/VHS, Max leads us through a number of Bible passages that show Christ experiencing the unique pressures and trials of life on earth. We don't have time to look at them all, but consider the following verses.

You may want to have participants read aloud, in turn, these passages and the ones following.

Mark 3:21 says:

> *When his family heard what was happening, they tried to take him home with them. "He's out of his mind," they said.* (NLT)

Mark 6:2–3 says:

> *"Where did this man get these things?"' they asked. "What's this wisdom that has been given him, that he even does miracles! Isn't this the carpenter? Isn't this Mary's son and the brother of James, Joseph, Judas and Simon? Aren't his sisters here with us?" And they took offense at him.* (NIV)

What do these passages reveal about Christ's life experience? Do you think Jesus had thick skin and a tough heart? Or do you think the experience of having his own family and close friends doubt him (and his sanity!) hurt his feelings?

How might these experiences make Jesus sympathetic to your own relational/familial trials?

Isaiah 53:2 describes the coming Messiah (Jesus) in this way:

He has no stately form or majesty that we should look upon Him, nor appearance that we should be attracted to Him. (NASB)

In the *Next Door Savior,* Max writes:

Jesus had . . . common looks. . . . Drop dead smile? Steal-your-breath physique? No. Heads didn't turn when Jesus passed. If he was anything like his peers, he had a broad peasant's face, dark olive skin, short curly hair, and a prominent nose. He stood five feet one inch tall and weighed around 110 pounds. Hardly worth a *GQ* cover. According to a third-century historian, Origen, "his body was small and ill-shapen and ignoble." (p. 14)

Is this a new thought to you? If what Max writes is true, if Jesus of Nazareth really *wasn't* much to look at, how could he possibly have been so popular with the masses?

Hebrews 2:17–18 says:

> *He had to enter into every detail of human life. Then, when he came before God as high priest to get rid of the people's sins, he would have already experienced it all himself—all the pain, all the testing—and would be able to help where help was needed.* (MSG)

"Every detail of human life" . . . except sin. How did Christ manage to enter our world and experience human existence fully—yet without sinning? Why was it necessary that Jesus *not* sin?

Mark 1:35 explains:

> *Early the next morning, while it was still dark, Jesus woke and left the house. He went to a lonely place, where he prayed.* (NCV)

Mark 6:31 says:

> *Then, because so many people were coming and going that they did not even have a chance to eat, he said to them, "Come with me by yourselves to a quiet place and get some rest."* (NIV)

Why do you think Jesus was so intentional about taking time for solitude and reflection—time alone with God the Father? What does this suggest to you?

Matthew 15:30–31 reports:

> *Great crowds came to him, bringing the lame, the blind, the crippled, the mute and many others, and laid them at his feet; and he healed them. The people were amazed when they saw the mute speaking, the crippled made well, the lame walking and the blind seeing. And they praised the God of Israel.* (NIV)

In Matthew 11:19, Jesus says:

> *The Son of Man came eating and drinking, and they say, "Here is a glutton and a drunkard, a friend of tax collectors and 'sinners.'" But wisdom is proved right by her actions.* (NIV)

What do these passages indicate about how Jesus lived, where he hung out, and the kinds of people with whom he associated?

Hebrews 2:18 states:

> *Because he himself suffered when he was tempted, he is able to help those who are being tempted.* (NIV)

The Amplified Bible renders it this way: "For because He Himself [in His humanity] has suffered in being tempted (tested and tried), He is able [immediately] to run to the cry of (assist, relieve) those who are being tempted and tested and tried [and who therefore are being exposed to suffering]."

When you are tired, discouraged, guilty, sad, or angry, do you *really* believe—in your heart of hearts—that Christ knows exactly how you feel and that he cares? Why or why not?

As we've read, Hebrews 2:18 refers to "all the pain . . . all the testing" that Jesus faced. In the DVD/VHS clip you watched, Max cites all kinds of tough trials and human emotions that Jesus faced. Which of the following connection points do you share with Christ? (Check all that apply.)

_____ A family tree with some bad apples/questionable characters

_____ Loneliness

_____ Discouragement

_____ Being from a nowhere hometown

_____ Raised by a single parent

_____ From a lower-income family

_____ Average looks

_____ Dealing with stressful leadership pressures

_____ People making constant demands on you

_____ A victim of false accusations

_____ Misunderstood by family and friends

_____ Hated and mistreated by the powerful

_____ Abandoned by friends

Which of these trials or struggles cause you the most pain and why?

Front Porch Story (10 to 15 minutes)
A Purpose for Pain—Courtney Connell

The testimony itself takes about five minutes.

This might be a good time to break into smaller groups (4 to 7 in each group) to discuss the testimony. Then, if you have time, group members could spend time praying for each other. Remember, however, that it will take a few minutes to move into and out of the groups.

The DVD/VHS clip of Courtney Connell is a powerful testimony to God's nearness when we experience loss.

In what ways is the Bible's revelation of a next door Savior powerful proof of God's willingness to get down in the trenches of life with us?

Courtney described an almost picture-perfect life that slowly unraveled. Can you relate? How so?

To borrow Courtney's words, what aspects of this study don't just "make you think" but "make you act"—that is, call for you to change?

How is it possible to be thankful for pain? Isn't this just a kind of denial?

What difficulties are you facing right now that your Christian brothers and sisters could help you bear and overcome?

Home Improvement (11 to 15 minutes)

With the questions that are more personal, you can have participants answer privately, writing in the space provided.

What would you say is your greatest trial or source of stress right now? Why? Based on what you've read and studied so far, what do you think Jesus might be saying to you?

Max observes:

> Jesus has been there. He experienced "all the pain . . . all the testing" (Hebrews
> 2:18 MSG). Jesus was angry enough to purge the temple, hungry enough to eat
> raw grain, distraught enough to weep in public, fun loving enough to be called
> a drunkard, winsome enough to attract kids, weary enough to sleep in a storm-
> bounced boat, poor enough to sleep on dirt and borrow a coin for a sermon
> illustration, radical enough to get kicked out of town, responsible enough to
> care for his mother, tempted enough to know the smell of Satan, and fearful
> enough to sweat blood. But why? Why would heaven's finest Son endure earth's
> toughest pain? So you would know that "He is able . . . to run to the cry of . . .
> those who are being tempted and tested and tried" (Hebrews 2:18 AMP).

Have you ever stopped to think of Jesus in this light?

John 1:12 affirms: "But to all who believed him and accepted him, he gave the
right to become children of God" (NLT). Though we all are God's *creatures*,
according to this verse, not everyone is a *child* of God.

What does this verse say about how a person becomes part of God's
family?

Optional Assignment: You may want to use these last three questions as the
assignment for the next week. Encourage everyone to pray for the people they
have listed.

Have you ever put your trust in Christ—that is, acknowledged Jesus
as the only One who can make you right with God and give you
eternal life? If so, describe that experience and how it has changed
your life.

If you have never done so, would you like to embrace Christ as your next door Savior right now? Write out a simple prayer that expresses your desire to know Christ and to follow him.

Write down the names of three people you intend to tell about your newfound devotion to Christ.

Community Connection

- Listen to "In the Garden/There Is None Like You" on the *Next Door Savior* CD.
- If you'd like to better understand Christ's death on the cross—its significance and its power to change lives—read Max's short book *Give It All to Him.*

Journaling Page

Session Four

Jesus . . . Near Enough to Touch

Lesson Goal: To know that Jesus loves us and wants the best for us: for-giveness, healing, and guidance. As a result of this session, participants will know that they can reach out to Christ and experience his power to heal their sorrow and pain.

Open House (10 to 12 minutes)

Play the "Next Door Savior" theme song as you begin.

Briefly review the last session before heading into this one. If you gave the assign-ment, ask how it went.

Let's do a little personal reflection. How would you best describe your rela-tionship with Jesus Christ right now?

_____ Skeptical seeker (You're not sure *what* to think!)

_____ Curious disciple (You're a learner, hungry to know more.)

_____ Devoted follower

_____ Other:

Add some detail to that description.

If you were granted the opportunity to go back in time and witness any of Jesus' miracles up close and personal, which one would you choose? Why?

When in your life have you felt the most desperate? What caused this state of hopelessness? What did you end up doing?

What situations, circumstances, and relationships in life concern you most right now? Are there any that really *haunt* you? Explain.

At Home with Max (17 to 22 minutes)

Show video segment four here. It will take about twelve minutes.

Max's teaching segment on the *Next Door Savior* DVD/VHS focuses on Christ's healing a woman with a serious, long-term medical condition, found in Mark 5:25–34 (NLT):

Have someone read this passage aloud. Be sure to ask the person beforehand, so he or she can review it.

> And there was a woman in the crowd who had had a hemorrhage for twelve years. She had suffered a great deal from many doctors through the years and had spent everything she had to pay them, but she had gotten no better. In fact, she was worse. She had heard about Jesus, so she came up behind him through the crowd and touched the fringe of his robe. For she thought to herself, "If I can just touch his clothing, I will be healed." Immediately the bleeding stopped, and she could feel that she had been healed!
>
> Jesus realized at once that healing power had gone out from him, so he turned around in the crowd and asked, "Who touched my clothes?"

His disciples said to him, "All this crowd is pressing around you. How can you ask, 'Who touched me?'"

But he kept on looking around to see who had done it. Then the frightened woman, trembling at the realization of what had happened to her, came and fell at his feet and told him what she had done. And he said to her, "Daughter, your faith has made you well. Go in peace. You have been healed."

Imagine struggling with anything for *twelve years!* Go back twelve years in your own life. Where were you then? What was your life like? How was it different?

What do you think this woman's twelve-year experience of a difficult medical condition must have been like?

How might this woman's life have turned out differently if the first or second doctor she had consulted (back in year one) had been able to get her condition under control? What does this suggest to you about God's ability to use brokenness in our lives to lead us to deeper blessing?

Look in Mark 5 at the words Jesus used responding to the woman: "Your faith has made you well"; "Go in peace"; "You have been healed." How do these sentiments fit with the mission that Jesus announced for himself in Luke 4:14–19?

Read this passage aloud.

The story of the bleeding woman represents a parenthesis within another story. A panicky, prominent synagogue official had just convinced Jesus to come quickly and save his dying daughter. The man's entourage then, on a time-sensitive, life or death mission, was interrupted by this anonymous bleeding woman (see Mark 5:21–25).

> Imagine being this religious leader with a dying daughter back home. How do you feel as Jesus leisurely stops to locate and tend to this lowly woman in the midst of a massive crowd?

> By any standards, Jesus lived a full, often jam-packed life. Yet he never seemed stressed, hurried, or frantic. Why do you think this was so? What was his secret? (Hint: See Mark 1:35–38; also John 8:29.)

Beforehand, ask individuals to read these passages aloud at this point in the session.

> What does this incident with the bleeding woman show you about the power of Jesus? About his compassion and care for *every* individual?

Front Porch Story (10 to 14 minutes)
Walking by Faith—Edward and Barbara Fidellow

The testimony will take about six minutes.

Watch Edward and Barbara Fidellow tell their story on the DVD/VHS.

> What in Edward's and Barbara's testimony was most powerful or poignant to you? Why?

The Fidellows experienced the death of a lifelong dream. When have you had a similar experience? What happened?

The Fidellows said that faith is not about getting what we want from God but about God getting what he wants from us—the character of Christ formed in us. In what ways and by what means do you sense God trying to mold you into a more Christlike person?

How does Edward's and Barbara's story encourage you in the midst of your own struggles?

Home Improvement (8 to 12 minutes)

The questions marked with an * are very personal, so you may want to have the group answer them privately. You can discuss the second question as a group.

*What would you say is the most desperate situation in your life right now—the concern that keeps you up at night and that you absolutely are powerless to fix? How does the biblical record of Christ healing the bleeding woman give you hope today?

Why do so many Christians remain blasé and unmoved when they read the Gospels? How do we avoid the trap of becoming numb to the amazing words and extraordinary works of Jesus?

Some people have a tendency to put Bible characters (even minor ones) in a special category and to view them as somehow *different*. Their situations were unique in history and their stories are interesting, but they're really irrelevant. That's an erroneous view. God wanted these snapshots of real life preserved in his Word—to give us an accurate picture of actual people who had undeniable encounters with heaven. His intent? To show us the kind of God he is and to birth in us the understanding that what he did *then*, he can do *now*.

  *What do you need—really *need*—from God right now? What is the deepest hunger of your heart?

  *This event from the life of Christ shows a next door Savior who is sensitive, searching, patient, and full of compassion. Is this *your* picture of Jesus? Why or why not?

  *When Christ left the earth, he commissioned his followers (the church) to be his body. According to the New Testament, we are his hands and mouth and feet in the world. So ponder for a moment: What people in your sphere of influence are feeling desperate and need to experience the loving touch of Christ? How specifically can *you* reach out to them this week?

  *Max points out that Jesus encouraged this hurting woman to tell him her story, the "whole truth." How long has it been since someone came alongside you with no agenda except to listen to your spiritual story? What can you do to be that kind of person to those God has placed in your life?

This question leads to the assignment of actually *doing* this during the next few days (that is, coming alongside someone with no agenda except to hear that person's heart, to listen to his or her spiritual story).

Community Connection

- Listen to Third Day's version of "Blessed Assurance" on the *Next Door Savior* CD.

- Check out Max Lucado's book *A Love Worth Giving*. It's a great challenge to let God's love fill you and then overflow into the lives of others.

Journaling Page

Session Five

Jesus . . . Strong Enough to Trust

Lesson Goal: To know that Jesus is God. As a result of this session, participants will understand that Jesus saw himself as God. There are only two options: accept him as God or reject him as a megalomaniac.

Open House (9 to 12 minutes)

Play the "Next Door Savior" theme song as you begin.

Briefly review the last session before heading into this one. If you gave the assignment, ask for reports.

What is the wildest, most bizarre religious belief you've ever heard someone express?

If people are reluctant to share, remind them of some of the bizarre cults and leaders that have drawn national attention over the years (for example, Jim Jones, David Koresh, and others).

What belief systems or religions do you know the most about? The least about? What spiritual views are gaining popularity in your city or region?

In your view, how is Christianity unique among the religions of the world?

At Home with Max (17 to 22 minutes)

Show video segment five here. It's about twelve minutes long.

On the *Next Door Savior* DVD/VHS, Max compares our world—with its myriad of spiritual ideas and philosophical beliefs—to a religious midway. Like carnival barkers, smiling gurus and slick-talking spiritual "experts" try to entice us to try their versions of enlightenment, their paths to heaven.

Amid all the clamor, however, there is this: Some two thousand years ago, a humble Galilean Rabbi quietly claimed to be divine. And not once did he discourage his followers from worshiping him. When we pause long enough to let that fact sink in, our hearts begin to race. Can it really be?

Consider this fascinating scene in Luke 9:28–36 (NIV):

Have everyone turn to this passage in their Bibles. They should follow along as you read it aloud.

About eight days after Jesus said this, he took Peter, John and James with him and went up onto a mountain to pray. As he was praying, the appearance of his face changed, and his clothes became as bright as a flash of lightning. Two men, Moses and Elijah, appeared in glorious splendor, talking with Jesus. They spoke about his departure, which he was about to bring to fulfillment at Jerusalem. Peter and his companions were very sleepy, but when they became fully awake, they saw his glory and the two men standing with him. As the men were leaving Jesus, Peter said to him, "Master, it is good for us to be here. Let us put up three shelters—one for you, one for Moses and one for Elijah." (He did not know what he was saying.)

While he was speaking, a cloud appeared and enveloped them and they were afraid as they entered the cloud. A voice came from the cloud, saying, "This is my Son, whom I have chosen; listen to him." When the voice had spoken, they found that Jesus was alone. The disciples kept this to themselves, and told no one at that time what they had seen.

What's going on here? Describe the change in Jesus.

Why did Moses and Elijah appear? Do you agree with Max that perhaps their purpose was to comfort Jesus? Why or why not?

What happened when Peter interrupted the proceedings with his idea about erecting monuments? How did God single out Christ as the One worthy of ultimate attention and honor and glory?

Consider these words from Jesus' lips, the claims he made about himself:

Beforehand, ask individuals to read these aloud at this time.

- "They all asked, 'Are you then the Son of God?' He replied, 'You are right in saying I am'" (Luke 22:70 NIV).
- "'I tell you the truth,' Jesus answered, 'before Abraham was born, I am!' At this, they picked up stones to stone him, but Jesus hid himself, slipping away from the temple grounds" (John 8:58–59 NIV).
- "Jesus answered, 'I am the way and the truth and the life. No one comes to the Father except through me'" (John 14:6 NIV).
- "Jesus answered: 'Don't you know me, Philip, even after I have been among you such a long time? Anyone who has seen me has seen the Father. How can you say, "Show us the Father"?'" (John 14:9 NIV).

How do you respond to such outlandish statements? Would you agree that Jesus saw himself as divine?

Max says, "Make no mistake, Jesus saw himself as God. He leaves us with two options: accept him as God, or reject him as a megalomaniac. There is no third alternative."

Author and scholar C. S. Lewis observed:

A man who was merely a man and said the sort of things Jesus said would not be a great moral teacher. He would either be a lunatic—on the level with a man

35

who says he is a poached egg—or else he would be the Devil of Hell. You can shut him up for a fool, you can spit at him and kill him as a demon; or you can fall at his feet and call him Lord and God. But let us not come with any patronizing nonsense about his being a great human teacher. He has not left that open to us. He did not intend to.

Can you think of any possibilities for who Jesus is other than lunatic, devil, or Lord?

Consider again what the apostle Paul wrote about the supremacy of Christ (we looked briefly at this passage in Session One):

Christ is the one through whom God created everything in heaven and earth. He made the things we can see and the things we can't see—kings, kingdoms, rulers, and authorities. Everything has been created through him and for him. He existed before everything else began, and he holds all creation together. Christ is the head of the church, which is his body. He is the first of all who will rise from the dead, so he is first in everything. For God in all his fullness was pleased to live in Christ, and by him God reconciled everything to himself. He made peace with everything in heaven and on earth by means of his blood on the cross. (Colossians 1:16–20 NLT)

How does this description elevate Christ over everything and everyone else? In what ways is Christ special and unique?

Where and when did you first realize the uniqueness of Christ? What happened? Or, are you still unsure about him?

Do you understand why Jesus can't simply be labeled a good man or a great moral teacher? How do his clear claims to be God eliminate those possibilities?

Do you see why—if Jesus really *is* God in the flesh—the Christian faith has to be viewed as the ultimate explanation of reality, and all the other major religions of the world must be wrong?

Front Porch Story (10 to 13 minutes)
One Day at a Time—Russ and Tammy Bookbinder

The testimony is about six minutes long.

Take a few minutes to view the testimony of Russ and Tammy Bookbinder on the DVD/VHS.

Russ was raised in a Jewish home and came to understand and believe that Jesus truly is Messiah. He married Tammy shortly after her diagnosis with multiple sclerosis. The Bookbinders have to trust God daily with Tammy's health. Life is a real struggle for them, yet they live with great hope and purpose as they rest in the truth of God's sovereignty and love.

What about the Bookbinders' story affects you most deeply?

What do you find most intriguing about their story?

Put yourself in their place. How would you respond? Would you be angry with God? Would you find it hard to trust him?

In what ways do you see God working, orchestrating, directing their lives? What about your life?

Home Improvement (9 to 13 minutes)

With what you know of Jesus Christ and the claims of the gospel, why would anyone look elsewhere for salvation and help and hope? To what do you attribute the popularity of fringe groups, New Age spirituality, and cults?

Are you crystal clear about who Jesus is? Have you trusted him to be your Savior? Are you sure you are God's child and that you have eternal life? On what do you base your beliefs?

A neighbor accuses you of being "narrow-minded" and "intolerant." He calls you a "religious bigot" for insisting that Jesus is the only way to God. (Actually, all you did was quote Christ himself—specifically, his words from John 14:6.) How would you defend yourself? Or *would* you?

Can we "argue people into God's kingdom"? Should we even try? (Hint: See 1 Peter 3:15.)

Apologetics is that branch of theology devoted to defending the claims of Christianity. The goal is to show that our faith is rooted in history and based on sound facts and reasons. Have you ever taken a course or read a book that explains *what* you believe and *why*? What are your biggest unanswered questions about God or the Christian faith?

How do you think differently and feel differently after this time of study and reflection? How do you intend to *act* differently? (Be specific.)

Optional Assignment: Have each member of the group research the beliefs of a cult or fringe religious group.

Community Connection

- Listen to "'Tis So Sweet to Trust in Jesus" on the *Next Door Savior* CD.
- If you have questions about the Christian faith and need a crash course in why it is rational to believe in Jesus, read the best-selling books by former atheist Lee Strobel, *The Case for Christ* and *The Case for Faith*.

Journaling Page

Session Six

Jesus . . . Carried Our Sins

Lesson Goal: To know that Jesus paid the penalty for our sins. As a result of this session, participants will know the meaning of the Cross and that all we must do is accept God's grace, his gift of salvation.

Open House (6 to 10 minutes)

Play the "Next Door Savior" theme song as you begin.

Briefly review the last session before heading into this one. If you gave the assignment, ask for volunteers to report on what they learned about certain cults and fringe religious groups.

When was the last time you did something really difficult and terribly scary—something you truly did *not* want to do? What was it? Why'd you do it? What happened in the end?

You may have seen a Passion Play of Jesus' crucifixion. Or perhaps you've watched an Easter presentation at church with Jesus hanging on the cross. How do such reenactments affect you? Do you come away feeling more loved? More guilty? More confused? Why?

At Home with Max (18 to 23 minutes)

Ask the question below before showing the video selection for this session.

So far, much of our study has focused on Christ as our *neighbor*—his coming to earth and identifying with our human dilemma. This session looks at Christ as our *Savior.*

What does the word *savior* mean to you?

Now show video segment six. It will take almost thirteen minutes.

What did Jesus do to make us acceptable to God?

For the answer to this question, we have to witness a brutal execution. It's not a scene for the squeamish. Here's how the Bible describes it:

> At noon the whole country was covered with darkness, which lasted for three hours. At about three o'clock Jesus cried out with a loud shout, "Eli, Eli, lema sabachthani?" which means, "My God, my God, why did you abandon me?" (Matthew 27:45–46 GNT)

Notice that the passage speaks of a thick darkness that descended on Calvary. In the Old Testament we read these prophetic words:

> "In that day," declares the Sovereign LORD,
> "I will make the sun go down at noon
>   and darken the earth in broad daylight.
> I will turn your religious feasts into mourning
>   and all your singing into weeping.
> I will make all of you wear sackcloth
>   and shave your heads.
> I will make that time like mourning for an only son
>   and the end of it like a bitter day." (Amos 8:9–10 NIV)

What do you think it means, this strange darkness that enshrouded Golgotha as Jesus hung on the cross (see Matthew 27:45)? The historian Dionysius is reported to have said, "Either the God of nature is suffering, or the machine of the world is tumbling into ruin." What did he mean?

If we rewind the video of Jesus' life a little more than three years, to that moment when he began his public ministry, we find John baptizing people in the Jordan and greeting Jesus with these words: "The next day he saw Jesus coming toward him and said, 'Behold, the Lamb of God who takes away the sin of the world!'" (John 1:29 NASB).

What did John mean by calling Jesus "the Lamb of God who takes away the sin of the world"?

Why did Jesus have to die? Or, put another way, what would have happened if Jesus had never made a perfect sacrifice for sin?

In Matthew 27:46, what did Jesus mean when he said, "My God, my God, why did you abandon me?"

These desperate words spoken by Christ from the cross are actually found in Psalm 22. Jesus was quoting David. Read Psalm 22. What is the significance of this repetition?

Have everyone turn to Psalm 22 and read it silently, or you read the psalm aloud while everyone follows along.

Look carefully at the following two passages:

> *The sun and moon will be darkened,*
> *and the stars no longer shine.*
> *The LORD will roar from Zion*
> *and thunder from Jerusalem;*
> *the earth and the sky will tremble.*
> *But the LORD will be a refuge for his people,*
> *a stronghold for the people of Israel.* (Joel 3:15–16 NIV)

> *About the ninth hour Jesus cried out in a loud voice, "Eloi, Eloi, lama sabachthani?"—which means, "My God, my God, why have you forsaken me?"* (Matthew 27:46 NIV)

Max notes the Joel prophecy of the Lord "roaring from Zion" and then points out Matthew's report that Jesus "cried out in a loud voice." He concludes that the reason Jesus screamed (or roared!) these haunting words is so that we will never have to.

What does Max mean by this?

The apostle Peter writes: "Christ carried our sins in his body on the cross so we would stop living for sin and start living for what is right. And you are healed because of his wounds" (1 Peter 2:24 NCV).

According to Peter, what are the consequences—both personal and universal, both immediate and long-term, both bad and good—of Christ's agonizing experience on the cross?

Of the various kinds of pain that Christ endured on the cross, which of the following do you think was probably the most piercing? Why?

- Physical—the cruelty of crucifixion
- Mental/Emotional—the indignity and loneliness of it all, the jeers of the crowd, his Father's abandonment
- Spiritual—becoming sin, bearing the judgment of the world

Christ's followers responded differently to his death. A few lingered at the foot of the cross, weeping. Many stood at a safe distance. Peter even denied knowing Jesus.

If you had been one of the disciples, which group do you suspect you might have been a part of?

Front Porch Story (12 to 15 minutes)
By the Grace of God—Missy Billingsley

The testimony is about six minutes long.

On the DVD/VHS, you watched Missy Billingsley tell a powerful personal story of her struggle with cancer and a leg amputation. Radiation treatments kept her from conceiving a child, but the Lord put adoption on the hearts of Missy and her husband. They went to the Ukraine to adopt one child and came home with three!

Some people push God away in hard, dark times, while others reach out for him. Why?

Missy's agonizing story eventually had a happy ending, but we all know that sometimes people die or they cannot adopt. How do those people and their loved ones keep clinging to God in the face of disappointment?

In what ways is Missy's testimony a story of God's grace?

Home Improvement (9 to 12 minutes)

Because these *Home Improvement* questions are rather personal, one option is to have everyone answer them privately. Then you could have each person find a partner with whom he or she could share some of their answers and personal concerns and pray for each other.

Describe a time in your life when you felt far away from God. Perhaps you were wrestling with guilt or loneliness or dealing with a tremendous trial. Would you say you felt *abandoned*? Left to go it alone? Jot down some phrases and feelings that describe that dark time.

Max concludes his short talk with these words:

See Christ on the cross? That's a gossiper hanging there. See Jesus? Embezzler. Liar. Bigot. See the crucified carpenter? He's a wife beater. Porn addict and murderer. See Bethlehem's boy? Call him by his other names—Adolf Hitler, Osama bin Laden, and Jeffrey Dahmer. . . . With hands nailed open, he invited God, "Treat me as you would treat them!" And God did. In an act that broke the heart of the Father, yet honored the holiness of heaven, sin-purging judgment flowed over the sinless Son of the ages.

How do you feel to see Christ linked with history's most evil men and associated with evil acts?

First Peter 2:24, a verse we looked at above, declares that Christ carried all our sins in his body. What does this mean to you today?

A lot of unchurched and irreligious people avoid God and steer clear of conversations about Jesus because they think God is out to get them or make their lives miserable. Is that the message you've been getting from the Bible passages we've looked at in the *Next Door Savior* study? How might these reminders of God's infinite love (and *especially* the vivid truth of this chapter) alter the way many of your non-Christian friends and neighbors view Jesus?

What are some steps you can take to be more mindful of God's love all during your day? What is one specific way you want to be different as a result of having worked through this lesson of the *Next Door Savior* study?

The assignment for this session is to continue to pray for the partner during the week.

Community Connection
- Listen to Warren Barfield's song "Live With Us" on the *Next Door Savior* CD.
- Another related book by Max Lucado is *Six Hours One Friday*. If you're interested in meditating more on the meaning of Christ's death, you will find this book very helpful.

Journaling Page

Session Seven

JESUS . . . SPEAKS FOR YOU

Lesson Goal: To understand that Jesus intercedes for us. As a result of this session, participants will choose to bring all their cares, concerns, and requests to Christ.

Open House (6 to 9 minutes)

Play the "Next Door Savior" theme song as you begin.

Briefly review the last session before heading into this one. Because of the nature of the assignment, simply remind them of it and thank those who actually did it.

Tell everyone to keep their books closed as you ask the questions for the *Open House* section. Thus, for the word associations, they should shout out the first words that come to mind instead of writing them down.

Who is the most famous or most powerful person you've ever had personal contact with? How did it happen? Tell the facts of the story.

Let's play the word association game. Jot down the first word or phrase that comes to mind when you see or hear the following terms:

sovereign

authority

omnipotent

infinite

king

advocate

At Home with Max (20 to 25 minutes)

Show video segment seven. It will take about fourteen minutes.

In his message on the *Next Door Savior* DVD/VHS, Max cites a number of Bible verses. Let's take a closer look at some of them.

Ask volunteers to read these verses aloud. They can read right from their books.

Romans 8:34 says:

> *Who is he that condemns? Christ Jesus, who died—more than that, who was raised to life—is at the right hand of God and is also interceding for us.* (NIV)

What is Christ is doing right now? How does this pledge make you feel?

Matthew 28:18 announces,

> *Then Jesus came to them and said, "All authority in heaven and on earth has been given to me."* (NIV)

Ephesians 1:21–23 explains:

> *Now he is far above any ruler or authority or power or leader or anything else in this world or in the world to come. And God has put all things under the authority of Christ, and he gave him this authority for the benefit of the church. And the church is his body; it is filled by Christ, who fills everything everywhere with his presence.* (NLT)

Reflect on how these passages describe Jesus. Do the statements seem to square with reality as you know it? In other words, does it *feel* most days as if Jesus is the ultimate authority over everything? Does it seem to you that Christ is running the show right now, controlling the universe? Why or why not?

Colossians 1:15–16 declares of Christ:

He is the image of the invisible God, the firstborn over all creation. For by him all things were created: things in heaven and on earth, visible and invisible, whether thrones or powers or rulers or authorities; all things were created by him and for him. (NIV)

What are the implications of the phrase that "all things were created by [Christ] and for him"? How does this fact affect your daily life and attitude?

Job 37:9–14 speaks of God's amazing power as seen in creation:

> *The tempest comes out from its chamber,*
> *the cold from the driving winds.*
> *The breath of God produces ice,*
> *and the broad waters become frozen.*
> *He loads the clouds with moisture;*
> *he scatters his lightning through them.*
> *At his direction they swirl around*
> *over the face of the whole earth*
> *to do whatever he commands them.*
> *He brings the clouds to punish men,*
> *or to water his earth and show his love.*
> *"Listen to this, Job;*
> *stop and consider God's wonders."* (NIV)

Which of God's natural wonders most fill you with awe and take your breath away? Why?

How does creation reflect God's power?

Now, with that backdrop, with those reminders firmly fixed in your mind, consider this bold statement from the pen of the apostle Paul: "I can do all things through Christ who strengthens me" (Philippians 4:13 NKJV).

Don't discuss the following question—ask it rhetorically.

Do you live with such confidence? Are you governed by a deep, abiding assurance that God is bigger than every problem you face?

First John 2:1 says:

My little children, I am writing these things to you so that you may not sin. And if anyone sins, we have an Advocate with the Father, Jesus Christ the righteous. (NASB)

What is an *advocate*? What does this suggest about Christ's role?

Front Porch Story (10 to 12 minutes)
Everyday Miracles—Pamela Culbertson

Watch the testimony of Pamela Culbertson on the DVD/VHS.

What are your overall impressions of Pamela's spiritual experience? Can you relate? Are you touched? Challenged? Inspired? How?

Pamela described the difficulty of rearing two autistic boys, and yet she exudes genuine peace and quiet joy. How is this possible?

What part does surrendering to the will of God play in getting through tough times?

Pamela spoke of appreciating the "little things." Why is this sometimes hard to do?

How do you think Pamela sees Jesus as her "next door Savior"?

Home Improvement (9 to 14 minutes)

Keep this section personal and private; that is, do not discuss these questions as a group. Instead, have participants work individually and privately. In the background, you may want to play "In the Garden" from the *Next Door Savior* CD.

Imagine Jesus showing up physically in your kitchen tomorrow morning. He wants to sit with you and have coffee and breakfast.

Based on what you've seen and heard in this series, what do you think he might say to *you*?

What would you like to say to him?

Calling to mind the words of Philippians 4:13—"I can do everything through him who gives me strength" (NIV)—what life situation is currently giving you the most trouble? For what specific "everything" do you need God's strength today?

Meditate for a few minutes on this passage:

Jesus understands every weakness of ours, because he was tempted in every way that we are. But he did not sin! So whenever we are in need, we should come bravely before the throne of our merciful God. There we will be treated with undeserved kindness, and we will find help. (Hebrews 4:15–16 CEV)

How can this small group stand with you and support you this week? In what specific ways can you "be Christ" to them as well?

Close in prayer.

Optional: You may want to pass out copies of the "One Anothers" at the beginning of this guide (after the Small Group Toolbox).

Community Connection

- Listen to "How Deep the Father's Love for Us" on the *Next Door Savior* CD.
- A book by Max Lucado that focuses on Christ's power to move us through life's hard times is *When God Whispers Your Name*. You might want to use it in your devotional times.

Journaling Page

Journaling Page

Session Eight

Jesus . . . Give It All to Him

Lesson Goal: To know that Christ wants to take away our failures and give us lasting joy. As a result of this session, those who have not yet put their faith in Christ will open themselves up to God's endless and unconditional love, and those weary believers who are still clinging to shame or destructive attitudes and habits will find release.

This session has a strong evangelistic message, so be prepared to follow up with those who respond.

Open House (*7 to 12 minutes*)

Play the "Next Door Savior" theme song as you begin.

You may want to begin by asking everyone what they have learned so far from the study.

What's the greatest present you have ever received? What's the best gift you have ever given?

*On a scale of 1 to 10, with 1 being "trapped and sad" and 10 being "free and filled with joy!" how would you assess your current spiritual condition? Why?

This question marked with an * is a very personal question, so either skip it in the discussion or have everyone answer it privately.

Have you ever been to a landfill? What was it like? What sights and smells did you experience?

At Home with Max (15 to 20 minutes)

Begin this section of the session with the first few questions instead of the DVD/VHS. The discussion will help prepare participants for Max's message.

This session uses the simple allegory of a trashman and a landfill to summarize what our next door Savior has done for us. Several Scripture passages form the foundation for this powerful story.

Let's look first at John 1:29–31. Here's some background: John the Baptist has been creating quite a ruckus with the religious establishment and giving hope to those who hunger and thirst for righteousness, when suddenly Jesus shows up:

> *The next day John saw Jesus coming toward him and said, "Look! There is the Lamb of God who takes away the sin of the world! He is the one I was talking about when I said, 'Soon a man is coming who is far greater than I am, for he existed long before I did.' I didn't know he was the one, but I have been baptizing with water in order to point him out to Israel."* (NLT)

Why do you think John the Baptist referred to Christ as "the Lamb of God who takes away the sin of the world"? What about that title/description would have been significant to the Jewish crowds gathered about to hear John preach?

A little bit of research shows that John was actually a few months older than Jesus. What do you think John meant when he said that Jesus "existed long before I did"?

On another occasion during his earthly life and ministry, Jesus called out to all who would listen, "Come to me, all you who are weary and burdened, and I will give you rest" (Matthew 11:28 NIV). Look around at your neighbors, coworkers, and friends. What things— trash—cause them to feel weary and burdened? What are the most common ways people try to find rest and relief?

Play the DVD/VHS clip for Session Eight here. It will take about nine minutes.

The apostle Paul was a man well acquainted with the "trash" of regrets and messing up. He had spent the entire first part of his life in a zealous and prideful (but futile) pursuit of religious perfection. Soon he directed his fanatical energies at eradicating both the message and the followers of Christianity. Then, unexpectedly, he met the resurrected Jesus, and his life was never the same. He experienced true forgiveness. He became an altogether different person.

In one of his letters, he summed up what happens each time someone encounters and embraces the life-changing grace of God as offered to us by Christ:

Now we look inside, and what we see is that anyone united with the Messiah gets a fresh start, is created new. The old life is gone; a new life burgeons! Look at it! All this comes from the God who settled the relationship between us and him, and then called us to settle our relationships with each other. God put the world square with himself through the Messiah, giving the world a fresh start by offering forgiveness of sins. God has given us the task of telling everyone what he is doing. We're Christ's representatives. God uses us to persuade men and women to drop their differences and enter into God's work of making things right between them. We're speaking for Christ himself now: Become friends with God; he's already a friend with you. How? you say. In Christ. God put the wrong on him who never did anything wrong, so we coudl be put right with God. (2 Corinthians 5:17–21 MSG, emphasis added)

How does Max's story of the trashman picture the possibility of a "fresh start" and a "new life" in Christ?

"How? you say. In Christ. God put the wrong on him who never did anything wrong, so we could be put right with God" (2 Corinthians 5:21). This verse beautifully summarizes the spiritual transaction that takes place when we turn in faith to Christ. What happens to our sins? What is the result for us?

In light of what Jesus has done for us, what does this passage say we should spend our lives doing?

Home Improvement (13 to 16 minutes)

You may want to break into smaller groups (four to seven in each) for the first part of this section. Remember that going into and out of groups takes a few minutes.

A psychiatrist on staff at a large mental hospital once remarked that the deepest problem of a huge percentage of his patients was plain old *guilt*—that they simply needed a sense of true forgiveness.

Why is guilt such a common problem? In your experience, how do most people end up handling their guilt?

What emotional, spiritual, or relational "garbage" do you find yourself lugging around? How does it weigh you down in life and rob you of joy? What is stopping you from giving this sack of "trash" to Christ?

When do you remember calling on Christ to take your sins and give you his forgiveness, his righteousness, his life?

Front Porch Story (10 to 12 minutes)

If you used small groups, bring everyone back together at this point.

This session has no DVD/VHS testimony. This would be a good opportunity for you to share how you came to faith in Christ, how you've given him your trash. Or you could have one or two group members share (be sure to contact them beforehand).

There is no special DVD/VHS testimony for this session. This would be a good time to listen to a friend's story of how he or she came to Christ, gave up their "trash," and experienced new life. What strikes you about this person's testimony?

Max concludes with these words:

You and I live in a trashy world. Unwanted garbage comes our way on a regular basis. We, too, have unanswered prayers and unfruitful dreams and unbelievable betrayals, do we not? Haven't you been handed a trash sack of mishaps and heartaches? May I ask, What are you going to do with it?

You have several options. You could hide it or even pretend it isn't there. But you won't fool anyone, and sooner or later it will start to stink. So what will you do?

It's time to take your bags to the street. It's Friday morning. Trash day. Just give your trash to him.

As you move into this prayer, encourage everyone to give Christ their trash, all of it.

Max suggests a prayer:

Dear Jesus,

For too long I have been carrying around the burden of my sin and all that accompanies it—sacks of shame, worry, pain, resentment, and failure. I have tried to live with the guilt and hurt, but they've grown heavy. I ache. I grieve. I feel crushed.

I realize that freedom begins by confessing my sin and giving it to you. You release me from my burden and take it to the cross. Now it's gone. Forever.

I once carried failure, but now I have forgiveness.

I once carried hate, but now I have hope.

I once carried fear, but now I have freedom.

Thank you for removing the garbage of my life. No longer is my life the same old story. Now, I have a new beginning. I am free because it is all in your hands. Amen.

What is keeping you from praying that prayer (or one like it)—from your heart—right now?

In conclusion, realize this: Whether you've given Jesus your trash for the first time or the hundredth time, you're free! The Savior is in your neighborhood, and he's made his home in your heart.

Encourage those who prayed this prayer for the first time—that is, those who just gave their lives to Christ, accepting his free gift of salvation—to speak with you afterward. Have some follow-up material you can give them and steer them to the next steps they should take.

Community Connection

- Purchase copies of *Give It All to Him* to give to friends, neighbors, and coworkers.
- Pray faithfully for those in your sphere of influence who are struggling under the weight of sin or shame or regret. Ask God to give them his grace and peace—both peace *with* God and the peace *of* God.

Journaling Page

Journaling Page

Prayer Journal

Use this space to write down personal or group prayer requests. The great thing about recording your own or your group's specific prayer requests and God's answers to these prayers is that you end up with a record of his wisdom, power, and faithfulness. Try it!

Date	Request	Date Answered & Details

Date	Request	Date Answered & Details

Also Available from Max Lucado

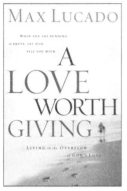

A Love Worth Giving

Finding it hard to love? Someone in your world is hard to forgive? Is patience an endangered species? Kindness a forgotten virtue? If so, you may have forgotten an essential first step. Living loved. God loves you. Personally. Powerfully. Passionately. Others have promised and failed. But God has promised and succeeded. He loves you with an unfailing love. And his love—if you let it—can fill you and leave you with a love worth giving.

Spanish edition available

America Looks Up

Since September 11, 2001, our nation has witnessed an incredible transformation in how we view life, security, and faith. In this small book, Max Lucado asks the questions on all our minds: Where is God in all of this? Can good really come from evil? And does God truly hear our prayers? Max encourages us, both as a nation and as individuals, to trust God with our hopes, fears, and questions.

An Angel's Story

Was the birth of Jesus a quietly profound event? Or could it have included heavenly battles, angel armies, and a scheming Satan? Come along as Lucado takes us on a journey into his imagination—pulling back the curtain as we see what might have taken place in *An Angel's Story* (previously titled *Cosmic Christmas*).

W Publishing Group™
www.wpublishinggroup.com

Spanish edition available

THE APPLAUSE OF HEAVEN

It is what you always dreamed of but never expected. It's having God as your dad, your biggest fan, and your best friend. It is having the King of Kings in your cheering section. It is hearing the applause of heaven. Max Lucado believes that the Beatitudes provide what we need to discover the joy of God. Much more than a how-to book on happiness, *The Applause of Heaven* is an encounter with the Source of Joy.

THE CHRISTMAS CHILD

A Chicago journalist finds himself in a small Texas town on Christmas eve. Lonely and alone, he encounters old faces and new facts . . . a handcarved manger, a father's guilt, a young girl's faith. The trip into the past holds his key to the future, and a scarlet cross shows him the way home.

Spanish edition available

A GENTLE THUNDER

How far do you want God to go in getting your attention? Don't answer too quickly. What if God moved you to another land? (As He did Abraham.) What if He called you out of retirement? (Remember Moses?) How about the voice of an angel or the bowel of a fish (Gideon and Jonah.) God does what it takes to get our attention. That's the message of this book: the relentless pursuit of God.

W PUBLISHING GROUP™
www.wpublishinggroup.com

THE GREAT HOUSE OF GOD

Using the Lord's Prayer as a floor plan for *The Great House of God*, Max Lucado introduces us to a God who desires his children to draw close to him. Warm your heart by the fire in the living room. Nourish your spirit in the kitchen. Step into the hallway and find forgiveness. No house is more complete, no foundation more solid. So come to the house built just for you, *The Great House of God*.

Spanish edition available

HE CHOSE THE NAILS
Available in Large Print

Christ's sacrifice has defined the very essence of mankind's faith for the past 2000 years. Now Max Lucado invites you to examine the cross, contemplate its purpose, and celebrate its significance. With his warm, caring style, Max examines the symbols surrounding Christ's crucifixion, revealing the claims of the cross and asserting that if they are true, then Christianity itself is true. The supporting evidence either makes the cross the single biggest hoax of all time, or the hope of all humanity.

Spanish edition available

HE DID THIS JUST FOR YOU

Building on stories and illustrations from the book *He Chose the Nails* by Max Lucado, *He Did This Just for You* is a 64-page evangelistic book that leads the readers through God's plan of salvation and offers an invitation to accept Christ. It's the perfect way to introduce the gospel to friends and acquaintances through Max Lucado's warm and easy to understand writing style. Experience God's grace and plan of salvation for the first time or use this booklet to share the message of hope with someone you know.

Spanish edition available

W PUBLISHING GROUP™
www.wpublishinggroup.com

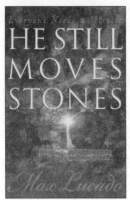

Spanish edition available

HE STILL MOVES STONES

Why does the Bible contain so many stories of hurting people? Though their situations vary, their conditions don't. They have nowhere to turn. Yet before their eyes stands a never-say-die Galilean who majors in stepping in when everyone else steps out. Lucado reminds us that the purpose of these portraits isn't to tell us what Jesus *did*—but rather to remind us what Jesus still *does*.

A HEART LIKE JESUS

The heart of Jesus is sacred, and the lessons and examples it provides to us are paramount in our daily mission to follow in His footsteps. Max Lucado poses the question "what if, for one day and night, your heart was replaced by the heart of Christ?" That thought-provoking question leads to many personal revelations demonstrating that we can recast our hearts to be more like that of Jesus.

Spanish edition available

IN THE EYE OF THE STORM

Come face-to-face with Jesus as He experiences more stress than any other day of his life aside from his crucifixion. Before the morning becomes evening, he has reason to weep, run, shout, curse, praise, and doubt. If you know what it means to be caught in life's storms . . . if you've ever ridden the roller coaster of sorrow and celebration . . . if you've ever wondered if God in heaven can relate to you on earth, then this book will encourage and inspire you.

W PUBLISHING GROUP™
www.wpublishinggroup.com

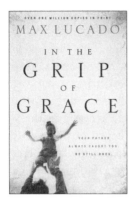

IN THE GRIP OF GRACE
Available in Large Print

Can anything separate us from the love of God? Can you drift too far? Wait too long? Out-sin the love of God? The answer is found in one of life's sweetest words—grace. Max Lucado shows how you can't fall beyond God's love. "God doesn't condone our sin, nor does He compromise His standard. Rather than dismiss our sin, He assumes our sin and incredibly, sentences Himself. God is still holy. Sin is still sin. And we are redeemed."

JUST FOR YOU

This artistic, full-color book will speak to your heart by combining the incredible images of The Visual Bible movies with the dynamic text of Lucado's classic book, *He Chose the Nails.* Prepare to experience the unmistakable power of the cross as you see how and why Jesus chose to undergo the ultimate sacrifice . . . just for you.

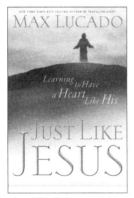

Spanish edition available

JUST LIKE JESUS
Available in Large Print

"What if, for one day, Jesus became you?" asks master storyteller Max Lucado. With this simple premise, Lucado tells how God loves you just the way you are, but He refuses to leave you there. He wants you to have a heart like His. He wants you to be just like Jesus.

W PUBLISHING GROUP™
www.wpublishinggroup.com

JUST LIKE JESUS DEVOTIONAL

This personal month-long journey with the Savior offers Scripture, practical devotions and application sessions to pattern one's life after Christ. Starting at day one, readers meet the Savior and find their way of thinking challenged. As readers begin to think more like Christ, they are challenged to put words into action as the journey escalates into a full force, radical retracing and renewal of what it means to be a follower of Christ.

NEXT DOOR SAVIOR

Master storyteller Max Lucado presents the life of Jesus Christ in stunning contrast, revealing the irresistible human qualities and the undeniably divine characteristics of Jesus. Lucado describes, as only he can, a Savior who is as approachable as a next-door neighbor, yet mighty enough to save humanity. Delving deeper into the life of Christ than ever before, Lucado melds the two distinct sides of Christ-human and God-into the complete likeness of our Lord.

Spanish edition available

Spanish edition available

TRAVELING LIGHT
Available in Large Print

No wonder we get so weary—we're worn out from carrying excess spiritual baggage. Wouldn't it be nice to lose some of those bags? That's the invitation of Max Lucado. With the twenty-third Psalm as our guide, we learn to release some of the burdens we were never intended to bear. Learn to lighten your load, as Max Lucado embraces what it really means to say, "The Lord is my Shepherd."

W PUBLISHING GROUP™
www.wpublishinggroup.com

TRAVELING LIGHT JOURNAL

Dare to slow down, take a break from the chaos of life and commit to meeting Christ like you never thought possible. Find yourself on a 30-day journey, led by Max Lucado, to better understand Psalm 23 and its power to teach you how to lighten your load. Each day includes a Scripture verse, a devotional excerpt, a short prayer, and space to write thoughts and prayers.

WHEN CHRIST COMES

Thoughts of the Second Coming are unsettling. Open graves and occupied clouds. Sins revealed and evil unveiled. Yet, for Max Lucado, the coming of Christ will be "the beginning of the very best." In *When Christ Comes*, Lucado shares how Christians can live in hope, confident in his comfort and peaceful in our preparations for His return.

Spanish edition available

WHEN GOD WHISPERS YOUR NAME
Available in Large Print

Do you find it hard to believe that the One who made everything keeps your name on His heart and on His lips? Did you realize that your name is written on the hand of God (Is. 49:16)? Perhaps you've never seen your name honored. And you can't remember when you heard it spoken with kindness. In this book, Lucado offers the inspiration to believe that God has already bought the ticket with your name on it.

Spanish edition available

W PUBLISHING GROUP™
www.wpublishinggroup.com